WILDERNESS SEARCH DOGS

By Dan Greenberg

Consultant: Wilma Melville, Founder
National Disaster Search Dog Foundation

BEARPORT
PUBLISHING COMPANY, INC.

New York, New York

Special thanks to Wilma Melville who founded the:
National Disaster Search Dog Foundation
206 N. Signal Street, Suite R
Ojai, CA 93023
(888) 4K9-HERO
www.SearchDogFoundation.org

The Search Dog Foundation is a not-for-profit organization that rescues dogs, gives them professional training, and partners them with firefighters to find people buried alive in disasters. They produce the most highly trained search dogs in the nation.

Design and production by Dawn Beard Creative and Octavo Design and Production, Inc.

Credits

Cover, Front (left), Carol J. Kaelson / Animals Animals Earth Scenes, (top right), (center right), AP / Wide World Photos, (bottom right), Syracuse Newspapers / David Lassman / The Image Works; Back (top), (center), AP / Wide World Photos, (bottom), Syracuse Newspapers / David Lassman / The Image Works. Title page. Carol J. Kaelson / Animals Animals Earth Scenes; 3, AP / Wide World Photos; 4-5, CORBIS; 5, AP / Wide World Photos; 6-7, Liz Otwell; 7, Frederick Florin // AFP / Getty Images; 8-9, Hulton Archive/Getty Images; 9, Bill Syrotuck / American Rescue Dog Association; 10-11, Ulrike Schnaz / Animals Animals Earth Scenes; 12-13, Image Source / Fotosearch; 13, Johan de Meester / Ardea; 14-15, Howard M. Paul / Emergency! Stock; 15, Nicole Baguette / Van Parys Media / CORBIS SYGMA; 16-17, AP / Wide World Photos; 17, Randy Batista / Media Image Photography; 18-19, 20, 21, AP / Wide World Photos; 22-23, The Star-Ledger; 23, Syracuse Newspapers / John Berry / The Image Works; 24, Gerard Lacz / Animals Animals; 25, Syracuse Newspapers / David Lassman / The Image Works; 26-27, AP / Wide World Photos; 27, AP / Wide World Photos; 28, Martin Leissl / VISUM / The Image Works; 29(top left), Photodisc / Fotosearch; 29(top right), Photospin.com; 29 (bottom left), (bottom right), Photodisc / Fotosearch.

Library of Congress Cataloging-in-Publication Data

Greenberg, Daniel A.
  Wilderness search dogs / by Dan Greenberg; consultant, Wilma Melville.
    p. cm.—(Dog heroes)
  Includes bibliographical references (p.   ) and index.
  ISBN 1-59716-019-9 (lib. bdg.) — ISBN 1-59716-042-3 (pbk.)
  1. Search dogs—Juvenile literature. 2. Rescue dogs—Juvenile literature. 3. Wilderness areas—Juvenile literature. I. Melville, Wilma. II. Title. III. Series.

  SF428.73.G74 2005
  636.7'0886—dc22

                        2004020755

For more information, write to Bearport Publishing Company, Inc., 101 Fifth Avenue, Suite 6R, New York, New York 10003. Printed in the United States of America.

1 2 3 4 5 6 7 8 9 10

Table of Contents

Lost!

A young boy named Jack wandered away from his house in Pennsylvania. When his parents learned he was missing, they looked for him everywhere. They couldn't find him. They called the police for help.

While the police searched the woods near Jack's house, the night got colder. Everyone began to worry that Jack couldn't stay warm. The faster they found him, the better. The police decided to call in a **wilderness** search and rescue team.

A wilderness search team

Wilderness search teams are made up of a dog and his handler.

5

Note: The name of the boy on pages 4–7 has been changed to protect his privacy.

Working Fast

Vicki Wooters arrived at Jack's house with her wilderness search dog named Tikki. The dog went right to work. Tikki sniffed around Jack's room to learn his **scent**. Then Vicki took Tikki outside so that the animal could search for the same smell.

As they headed into the woods, Tikki raced ahead of Vicki. The dog's nose was near the ground, sniffing. Suddenly, Tikki's head shot up. Vicki heard barking. Then she heard a small voice. It was Jack!

Vicki ran over to Tikki and Jack. She wrapped Jack in a blanket. He was safe.

Dogs are used for wilderness searches in many countries. In 2004, this team looked for a 14-year-old girl lost in a forest in France.

Wilderness search dogs use their noses, not their eyes, to search for missing people.

Tikki resting after a hard day of work

Ready to Help

Dogs have been used to find missing people for a long time. As far back as the 1500s, bloodhounds were used to hunt down people who escaped from prison. Later on, Saint Bernards were used to find people lost in the snowy mountains of Europe.

In the 1960s, Bill and Jean Syrotuck of Seattle, Washington, began training dogs to do rescue work. The Syrotucks soon founded the American Rescue Dog Association. Today, there are more than 300 dog search and rescue groups. These groups have saved hundreds of lives.

Jean Syrotuck

In the early 1800s, a Saint Bernard named Barry saved 42 people lost in the mountains of Europe.

1886 - Two Saint Bernards rescue an injured climber they found in the snow.

The Best Breeds

What kinds of dogs work best on a wilderness search and rescue team? Almost any dog can be trained. Larger **breeds**, however, are used more often than small dogs.

Border collie

Common wilderness rescue breeds include golden retrievers, Labrador retrievers, German shepherds, and Border collies.

Larger animals are better at wilderness rescues because they are stronger. Their longer legs help them run fast over rough ground. When in good **condition**, these dogs can also run for a long time without getting tired. They can keep going when a search lasts for several days.

Growing Up

Wilderness search dogs start training at a young age. **Trainers** look for puppies that are brave, **eager**, and have lots of energy.

The trainer tests each puppy by tossing him a toy. He wants the animal to chase the toy, grab it, and not let go. If the puppy does all these things, then he may make a good search dog.

Trainers don't use food as treats. They use play. After the animal has found someone, he might be rewarded with a game of fetch. Trainers want to teach the dog that making a rescue is fun.

A wilderness search dog learns **commands** such as seek, stay, leave, fetch, and out. Each command has its own hand signal.

These German shepherd puppies are usually too busy to pose for pictures.

Tracking Dogs

Some wilderness search dogs are tracking dogs. They learn to search by following a person's scent. They are taught this skill when they are puppies. To help the animals learn to track, the trainers play hide-and-seek with them.

While the trainer hides, the puppy is given a scent item to smell. The item, for example, could be a shirt that has the trainer's smell on it. Then the puppy uses his nose to find where the person is hiding. The trainer and the puppy play this game over and over.

This bloodhound is given a scent item to smell.

Scent items, such as a sock or glove, are kept in plastic bags. An item is only useful if no one but the owner has touched it.

Pockets was one of the first wilderness search dogs to work in Colorado.

On the Move

When a wilderness search dog starts tracking, he zigzags through the forest. He moves his nose up and down through the air as he follows the smell. At times, his nose stays near the ground, pulling up the scent.

After the dog finds the missing person, the handler checks the person to make sure he or she is healthy. Then the dog gets a reward. Some handlers pet their dogs. Others play with them. Caroline Hebard, a well-known trainer, gives her dog a stick to chew on.

Caroline Hebard with her wilderness search dog Lasso

Teams try to search with the wind coming at them from the side. The wind blows the scent directly onto the dog's nose.

Kathy Doty and her dog Summer search for a small boy in Mississippi.

Air Scenting

Other wilderness dogs learn to search by air scenting. In this kind of search, the dog is not given a scent item. He starts by putting his nose high and then low in the air. He's hunting for any live person in the area. The dog can hunt this way because he has a great sense of smell. It's 1,000 times stronger than our own.

How do dogs track a person's smell? Everyone loses skin **cells** that float in the air. People can't see the cells. Dogs can pick up the scent of a few cells over a wide area.

Dogs can pick up the scent of a person or a sandwich from as far as a mile away.

On the Job

Even on his first real search, a wilderness dog knows what to do. There are many people in the search area. Most of these people are strangers. The dog goes around and gives each person a sharp sniff.

After a tsunami hit Papua New Guinea in 1998, this search team from Florida flew in to help search for survivors.

Soon, the dog knows the scent of everybody in the group. Now he can search the forest for any scent that he doesn't know. A new scent may belong to the missing person.

A well-trained dog can track a human scent even if the smell is 10 days old.

This policeman and his dog are on a wilderness search.

Dogs to the Rescue

Wilderness search dogs come to the rescue during any kind of weather. Often, searches take place late in the day because the air is cooler. Cool air causes scents to stay near the ground. It's easier for a dog to smell a scent that is close to the ground.

RESCUE

Aly, during a training exercise

It's often after dark when hikers are reported missing, so some searches take place at night. Caroline Hebard and her dog, Aly, once looked for a group of children who were lost while hiking. At 2 o'clock in the morning, Aly found the group **huddled** together in the cold.

Wilderness search dogs can even use their great sense of smell to find people missing in rivers. Here, Azu "sniffs" for a missing fisherman.

Sometimes it's easier to find people in warm weather than in cold weather. People sweat more in warm weather, giving off lots of skin cells for the dogs to smell.

23

Danger on the Job

Wilderness search dogs work in all kinds of dangerous places. They might, for example, even need to be lowered by a helicopter to find a missing person.

Sometimes the dogs get hurt. After each search, the handler checks his **partner**. Has he cut himself on a hidden rock? Has he hurt his paw by stepping in a hole? The handler will treat any **wounds**.

Caroline Hebard once climbed down a cliff carrying her 100-pound wilderness dog who had been hurt.

RESCUE

Handlers, such as Rick Reardon, make sure their wilderness search dogs stay safe.

Proud and Brave

Search and rescue teams take great **pride** in their work. Every year, teams go to meetings where they get together with other handlers and their dogs. At the meetings, the handlers learn the latest ways to train their dogs. They also hear about new tools that might help them find missing people faster.

Being a wilderness search and rescue dog is hard work. The dogs train for many months. They must be ready to head into the woods at a moment's notice. These brave animals love their work. There is nothing they would rather do than search.

Even the army uses search and rescue dogs. Buster, shown here with Sergeant Danny Morgan (his handler), received an award in 2003 for his work during the war in Iraq.

One wilderness search and rescue dog can cover more ground than 12 human searchers.

Rescue dogs and their handlers from the Connecticut Canine Search and Rescue group train for water rescues at Mystic Seaport in Connecticut.

Just the Facts

- There are two different kinds of wilderness search and rescue dogs: tracking dogs and air-scenting dogs.

- Wilderness search dogs can be male or female.

- Cells for the sense of smell take up one-eighth of a dog's brain.

- Rain can sometimes make a scent stronger. Too much rain, however, can wash away a scent.

- In the United States, there are search and rescue groups in all 50 states.

- People started keeping dogs as pets 14,000 years ago.

A wilderness search team during a training exercise

golden retriever

Border collie

Labrador retriever

German shepherd

breeds (BREEDZ) types of a certain animal

cells (SELZ) the basic, microscopic parts of an animal or plant

commands (kuh-MANDZ) instructions to be obeyed; orders

condition (kuhn-DISH-uhn) general health or physical fitness; shape

eager (EE-gur) wanting very much

handler (HAND-lur) someone who trains and works with animals

huddled (HUHD-uhld) gathered together in a close group

partner (PART-nur) one of two or more people who do something together

pride (PRIDE) a feeling of worth that comes from what someone has achieved or can do

scent (SENT) the smell of an animal or person

trainers (TRAYN-urz) people who teach other people or animals how to do something

wilderness (WIL-dur-ness) an area of land where there are trees and animals but usually no people

wounds (WOONDZ) injuries to the body in which the skin is cut or torn

Bibliography

American Rescue Dog Association. *Search and Rescue Dogs: Training the K9 Hero.* New York, NY: Howell Book House (2002).

Bulanda, Susan. *Ready! The Training of the Search and Rescue Dog.* Portland, OR: Doral Publishing (1995).

Hebard, Caroline, and Hank Whittemore. *So That Others May Live.* New York, NY: Bantam (1995).

Patent, Dorothy Hinshaw. *Hugger to the Rescue.* New York, NY: Dutton (1994).

Snovak, Angela Eaton. *Guide to Search and Rescue Dogs.* Hauppauge, NY: Barron's Educational Publishing (2004).

Read More

Jackson, Donna M. *Hero Dogs: Courageous Canines in Action.* New York, NY: Megan Tingley Publishing (2003).

Portman, Dale. *Rescue Dogs: An Amazing Stories Book.* Canmore, Alberta, Canada: Altitude Publishing (2003).

Presnall, Judith Janda. *Rescue Dogs.* San Diego, CA: KidHaven Press (2002).

Ring, Elizabeth. *Search and Rescue Dogs: Expert Trackers and Trailers.* Brookfield, CT: Millbrook Press (1994).

Shields, Scott, and Nancy M. West. *Bear: Heart of a Hero.* Thornwood, NY: Hero Dog Publications (2003).

Learn More Online

Visit these Web sites to learn more about wilderness search dogs:

www.ardainc.org

www.csar.org

www.dawgs.org

www.sardogs.org

About the Author

Dan Greenberg is the author of books on many different topics.
His books on animals include titles about whales, dolphins, wolves, spiders,
frogs, leopards, lizards, chimpanzees, and now dogs.